Kathleen Wiegner
Country Western
Breakdown

THE CROSSING PRESS, TRUMANSBURG, NEW YORK 14886

For Christine: who grows

ACKNOWLEDGEMENTS

"Moral Implications of a Landscape," "The Fears,"
Shoveling Snow at Night," Proteus," "God High,"
Northern Cross," "My card is the Ace of Cups," and
"Arriving at the Edge of America" appeared in *Northeast.*

"Country Western Breakdown," "The meat goes bad in a
day," "The Mother of Us All," Bridgit Bardot: Soured
Recluse," "Hard Mornings (3)," "Keeping Secrets,"
"Telling Rosella About My Hands," and "Driving North,"
in *Stations II.*

Other poems appeared in the following magazines:
*Beloit Poetry Journal,The Minnesota Review, Hierophant,
Love/Woman, Amalgamated Holding Company, Tempest,
The Sensuous President by 'K.'*

Anthologies: "Still Life" and "Watching an Old Love
Story" first appeared in *Brewing: 20 Milwaukee Poets.*
"For the Woman Who Asked Me If I Believe in God,"
and "Silver Dollar," first appeared in *Mountain Moving
Day.* "Something to Do With It," "I Want to be Beautiful,"
and "Hard Mornings (1) and (2)" first appeared in *This
Book Has No Title.* "Duck Ground," and "Autobiography,"
in *New Poems Out of Wisconsin.*

Cover designed by Gene Messick
Photo on title page by Dick Richards

It looked as if a night of dark intent
was coming, and not only a night, an age.
Someone had better be prepared for rage.
There would be more than ocean-water broken
Before God's last *Put out the Light* was spoken.

Robert Frost, "Once by the Pacific"

CONTENTS

Watching An Old Love Story

CHRONICLES OF THE ICE AGE

DRIVING NORTH

There is now only one direction
left to go,
        when I say it
we are more quiet than the radio
whispering with the strange voices
of Nashville or St. Louis.

                Everyone
at the truck stop stares
into a coffee cup.
Tired eyes, the lights
               there
like snow
springing at the windshield.

Walking back late to our motel
I see people motionless
in their lighted living rooms
snow up to their windows
the fields and roads rigid with
snow, silence of dead stars
overflows our room
drifts from the ceiling into my
sleep.
          And
there is no end to it.
The morning
sun on ice
we crush under us
but leave no trace.

Driving north
farm news on the radio,
                    I think
of cows' bodies steaming
before letting down
milk at dawn.

The eskimos have a hundred
names for snow,
naming its quiet moods,
its times of danger.
Crying the names of the snow,
we will still die of this cold
to lie like the faithful couples
carved on cathedral tombs.

THE MORAL IMPLICATIONS
OF A LANDSCAPE

First, there is the road
ahead, but more snow,
more trees edging horizons
beyond highway 80,
landscapes enough
to answer any question.

Then there is poetry,
erecting a baroque wilderness
of meaning, a thousand trees,
a thousand branches
where each bird in the ten
thousand twigs
sings the note we wait for.

Now a bird breaks cover high over the road,
hesitant, caught
by my alternatives.
The way he flies
answers only the direction
of his flight.

I KNOW

I know myself inside out. The tiny camera
that passes down my throat makes me gag.
But the picture comes back in true color.

I know that it is 2 a.m. and you are in bed
with someone. I know it from your voice on the phone.
I know how you will touch her, what you will say.

I can see my lungs balloon and collapse.
I can see your body rising and falling,
shadowing her face. That is your style,

why I am always in shadow, entering and leaving
you like some powerless ghost that only rattles
the doorknob. My guts at least are clear.

I will sit here with this late movie
until you are sleeping. But your arm
still holds her like an empty bottle.

So we are drinking together then,
our heads aching. My stomach is filled
with broken bottles, ground glass in my arteries.

Tomorrow I will ask what you did last night.
You will say, and I will say, "I know,"
knowing everything, as if I understood.

My pictures of hell are slashed organs
and your hand in her hair. Eve bites the apple
over and over like a slipped film reel.

Somewhere I heard or read, they took this monkey
cut off his head, burned away flesh from bone.
Scientifically, they said, he could not know.

STILL LIFE

It is the worst time,
the time so stuffed
to keep it quiet, as the
child, moves slowly with
the same bored and cranky
pace, they eat indifferently,
what she cooks indifferently,
T.V. set on the end of the table,
waiting for the next step
in the ritual, waiting
for the father, who may
or may not come, who
they do not even mention, there
may not be a father;
there is no way of knowing
whether they wait for that
or merely for the time to end,
the day to close over them,
mercifully. We know only
that they have this. And
it is not enough.

THE FEARS

Someone has hung
windchimes
that ring louder
in winter,
brown wooden bells
knocking the harsh edge
off sleep with their
oriental precision.

Upstairs the T.V.
says morning mass,

SUNDAY MORNING NOW

east and west blessing
over my head.

Count your blessings,
I say. Count your bones.

Instead I count my
different fears.

One. That night has sucked
out my heartbeat.

No. There. It has clicked
in, dependable, getting
things warm for rising.

Today, I vow,
I will not count them
past ten.
        Stick
to the important ones.
Well, I'm still laying down
heartbeats. Get on to
number

Two.

FOUR POEMS FOR CHRISTINE
MY DAUGHTER

1. Duck Ground

Drive slowly,
duck feeding area,
late for ducks this far north
and winter closing in.

All summer I moved slowly,
tangled in your smallness,
the park shifting into the deep shade
of ripe fruit and ducks moving
with gentleness to take bread
from your hand in my hand.

Scattering as I approach
through children who
lately walked through ducks
and pigeons with bread
and stones for the darkening late water,

I know they sense your absence
with winter closing in,
scattering me
with the sudden wings of their leaving.

2. Shoveling Snow at Night

Far off, she works
her rite, marks
shovelwide across
the lawn, does
not think it strange.

Black night, white lawn,
and her small red coat
diminished by their
absolutes, she is yet
wonderful, fine
as glass figures.
We wonder
that so much life
can be reproduced,
such detail rendered
in so small a scale.

I am not afraid
for her, barely
seen against the dark
hedge; standing clear,
lighted porch, I can be seen.
It is all she seems to need.

It is enough to be here,
calling occasionally,
she does not even mention
her monsters.
They are not here
now. She is making a path
between us. No one else
will walk here after she
follows me in.

3. Sick Watch

How often I said
my little doll.
Now her white
hands flutter
then lapse. She lies broken
as if dropped
from a great height.

Now all the cups
show their stained cracks,
the sofa threadbare,
burns on the rug,
paint chipped,
chair back wobbles,

the paper pasted over
the broken door pane
whispers. She rustles
like a burning leaf.

Careless, I accuse
myself with life,
forever watching the wreckage.
Her wagon left in the rain
softens. (Things I
did not know
were worth so much!)
All over are signs
from cheap souvenir shops:
You Must Pay for Everything
You Break.

4. Nightmare

She cries out
breaking the darkness
between our dreams.

She has dropped the reins
and reality plunges
out of control.

She is afraid of the electric fan
we keep in the kitchen,
the sound and flashing blades,

and in her dream
it walked into her room
and began to turn.

I can lock it in the closet.
I can leave the small light burning.
But something dark has touched her.
Finally, I can only lie awake, listening.

AT THIS TIME

Fog fills up
the spaces, becomes
that failed vision,
that entropy when
everything sags in
upon itself,
clogs and chokes,
lights move from shadow
into shadow like bad dreams.

A few blocks from home
Christine says the house
must be a mile away
because we cannot see it.

FOR THE WOMAN WHO ASKED ME
IF I BELIEVE IN GOD AND IF I PRAY

Yes, lady, in the bright red suit
and careful grey hair, coming out
of nowhere one Sunday afternoon,
coming at me, I have taught my daughter
that God is everywhere
> even when she laughs
> saying, "in my toast,"
> taking a big bite.

God, lady, like sex, is something you can't avoid
so you do what you can.
Sometimes she thinks God is in a big airplane
> digging the clouds
> and an occasional glimpse of the ground.

But prayer.
That we haven't talked about because yes, lady,
I pray, like Christ himself prayed, in the garden,
that last night, knowing what lay before,
knowing but still hoping there was a way out,
praying for a way out, in sweat and darkness
he prayed. Not the way they teach you:
> God bless mommy, daddy,
> Bobbie and Jane.
> And please, God, let me
> have a pony for my birthday.

No one teaches you the other, the one you say
sweating in the dark, the only one you really need,
hopeless and still hoping, on your knees,
pinned there by what you know but still saying
> "let it pass."

No, I will not teach my daughter how to pray.
She will learn it herself. When the time comes.

CUNNING OF THE MAD PEOPLE

Weather
for instance
has it. We need an entire
organization to keep track
of where it's at.

What is the report today?
Sunny? Or more rain?
Call back in an hour
in case of change.

Or don't talk at all,
it confuses them more,
that breathing on the line
as if the next word
would be obscene.

Cultivating the superficial
anxieties, newspaper pictures,
eyes brooding like hostile girls
waiting to be asked to dance.
Who then refuse.

The cunning ones
have their own hypnosis.
They can lure children through
the roughest margins of the park
sure the next turn
will unearth the right clue
and the prize.

Now if you were in India
you would know what the snake
is doing, hear the mongoose shriek,
and refuse to believe the rope rising
skyward, right before your eyes,
as solid as a young tree.

PROTEUS

Well, here I am and
he, there, we have
this act. Oh I know
his tricks; we know
each other well enough.

Once when I had him
down he changed to
a child, crying in pain,
crying "mother help me"
and I believed him
until he had his hand
at my throat. Or once
as I held him, he grew
young and white
as a boy, whispering
"please, do it now."
I could not refuse
and lost my advantage.

Sometimes before we go on
he counsels, "it is political
to lose, the crowd is on
my side, give them what
they want and we can be
in the big time."
Then he changes to money,
to love, thousands of hands
applauding our carefully
worked out act.

People gossip, saying
we sleep together, that
we really love each other,
that our fights are never real.
They do not understand
that he never sleeps,
but stands in the corner all night
watching my dreams.

GOD HIGH

Cupboards that cannot be reached
except with chairs,
tipping forward and feeling
with fingertips

where did I put it?

Lost in the space
above my eyes.

Someone says that a
teacher should make
the student stand on tiptoe
reaching for the next
level

and the great blue sky
of Wyoming,
65 miles to the next
services, levels of
grass, wire, distant
big horn mountains

when will we get there?

Lying awake on some peak
and still the big black sky
crowded with stars, and I

tipping forward and groping
for lost objects,
knowing that the nearest
star light, millions of miles
to the next service station,
may have already exploded, may
even have vanished
before my fingers
could reach it.

COUNTRY WESTERN BREAKDOWN

NUMEROLOGY

Seven wonders do not make the world,
seven seas, seven continents don't.
Seven wounds do not make a god,
not seven mysteries, seven stations.
Seven swords through the heart
do not make a mother. Not likely.

Seven veils do not hide the mystery.
Seven plagues are not the disease.
No gold in the seven cities
not even seven cities
       seven come eleven
       it keeps on coming.
Seven labors do not quiet the gods.
Seven years may be feast or famine.
Seven years win a bride, the wrong one.
       seven come eleven
       coming, coming.
Seven sins do not make a sinner.
The good man takes seven sacraments
yet he falls, seven times a day.
And he falls, he falls,
       seven times, seven times
falling through the hole of the infinite,
the true mystical number,
not seven. Not enough. Not likely.

APOLOGY

if we had not come
to live in the jungle,
we would not have seen
the dead horse in the road;
the armless beggar playing
paper and comb,
tapping his feet together;
the dark woman and her baby
hiding from a photograph.
Just remember your mother
sent you away because she too
became a tiger one night
and could not change back
in the morning.
         Such things
happen here when it rains.
A dog has lain dead in
the road for two days now
and I have done nothing
because you are not here to notice.

TRUCK STOP (1)

Counterman said, "you some kind
of hippie," because she
had gold hoops in her ears
and her hair tied with a scarf;
said, "we had two of them
in here last week,
girl and her guy camping
together, wanting free soup.
I said, 'listen, he
can work, can't he, just
stop giving him all that
free stuff and get him to
settle down, make you $40 a week
construction.' She said, 'we
don't sleep together we just
travel around,' but you know that's
crap. Say, maybe you're a gypsy
and can tell my fortune."
She looked at his hand,
said his love life looked
pretty wild, watching the set
lips of his wife flipping
eggs on the back grill.

THE MEAT GOES BAD IN A DAY

The meat goes bad in a day
because it is not well blooded
so we eat blood
everyday, we eat blood
in everything
blood of the poor,
blood of the wooden Christ
scourged and crucified
red in the decayed hollows
of every dark church,
blood on the knees
that scrape from plaza to altar
      here Guadalope,
      Virgin, patroness,
we honor you with blood.
After a bad kill
blood pours from the bull's mouth
like an offering, hearts still smoke
on the old altars, priests' hands
bloody, hair stiff with dried blood.

      Crazy country,
you pelican, slashing yourself
to feed your children blood
so they will never unlearn
that warm salt taste.
Carried home from market,
heaved over a shoulder,
the pig screams against this outrage
and shits in the street.

TRUCK STOP (2)

"I'm driving to Indiana next
week, pick up some stuff for
Devlin, going to take my 12 gauge
because we're going through
Chicago and you never know
when you might have to shoot
one of them."
Woman behind the counter said:
"ya, there's a lot of them
out there," leaning against
the calendar picture of
St. Mark's Cathedral which he thought
looked a lot like the Boise
State Capital
until she told him otherwise.

AT YAGUL

The old hawk god
still buffets above
the quiet ruin,
still rides supreme
the living current
then hangs as still
as ancient stone.
Below the earth stretches
out, all innocent
and green as among
the high and ancient places
we see him plunge
toward some hidden
violence and ascend.

TRUCK STOP (3)

He was wearing his girl's
jacket, worried because
they had had to split up and
the two drivers had promised
to keep their rigs together.
Then paying for his coffee
from her billfold,
a girl's name on the
driver's license, they
took him out back and
beat the shit out of him.
Mae called the highway cops
who listened and
then drove on.

COUNTRY WESTERN BREAKDOWN

The dried gourd seeds rattle
in Lucy's hand, she shakes it
for the crying child, she
rattles from tensions
that drive her staggering
from the oven to the phone.
Bruce's head rattles from wine
and hatred, warning
that he is ready to strike.

And later, standing on the deserted road,
drunk, car broken down,
trying to flag a ride,

he pulls out his revolver
and begins shooting at the cars.

HARD MORNINGS (1)

You would take
everything
I had

and say
you'd earned it

with your
young body
and occasional
concern

as if it were hard.

At times
you stand
at the bedroom
window excited
by the girls' legs
flashing in the street

as if I had not
been with you
all night
long.

One time
you got excited
just talking
about them,

God, you said,
those short skirts
and I was lying
beside you
with nothing on.

SILVER DOLLAR

A woman never knows what a good man she's got
never knows what a good man is
maybe like her father only
he drinks less,
maybe like her first love only
more faithful,
maybe like her second love only
more loving,
maybe like her last love only

a woman never knows
a silver dollar rolls
                because it's
                round
never knows what a good man's she's got
never knows what a good man is
never knows
the silver dollar rolls
because it's round
because
                silver dollar goes
                from hand to hand
                because it's round
never knows
never knows
goes
from man to man.

HARD MORNINGS (2)

Black sunshine
in a cool black glass

it shines

mother said a man won't
love you if he knows

you're loose sugar
not the tight wrapped kind.

Father said a man won't
buy the cow
when he can get milk
through the fence,

but anyhow.

Black sun light
it shines
in the window
on the floor

can't remember when
I last opened the
door to anyone.

One day last week I
painted the whole damn
room white, opened
the window and the
black
sun
light
shined in

shut it down.
Tight.
O, I could love you
but
no dice.

THE MOTHER OF US ALL

One old woman was mother of us all
fed us on tales as soon as we could crawl
    sugar and spice
    everything nice
    that's what little girls
    is made of
One old man was father of us all
come on boys, let's go down
    catch us a little tail
    work it around
    blow your horns, call your dogs
    catch a pretty little ground hog.
Snips and snails, puppy dog tails
that's what little boys
is made of, laughed ma.
Well,
up come Joe with a snigger and grin
groundhog gravy all over his chin

and
up come John, happy as a crane,
swore he'd even eat the brains

up come pa, saying save the hide
make the best shoe strings you ever tied

up come momma, saying give me some too
I'll make another groundhog, good as new.

She's a clever woman. Always busy.
Can make something out of nothing
or nothing out of something.
Comes easy.
Been doing it all her life.

HARD MORNINGS (3)

You wake up hard
and slow

like we were
back at it

you can love me
that way
anytime

but when you
hold me
to hurt me
hard and slow

I can't ask you
anything just

see me bleed.

And you say
good
and you say
good morning
every morning

pushing my
back to the wall.

Your hands are bright
as razors
slitting the morning open
for one last look
as if you were
the only one
who had died.

THE GENTLE LADIES

I.

I have a friend who says
he'll love me when my husband leaves me
and my body's bad.
                    My friend
the time is now. The mirror shows
a woman with no other miracles left,
a body that has borne a child
and one man for nine years,
that walks like the water carriers,
steadily, so as not to dislodge the load.

But the boy I love sleeps with girls
whose breasts cling to them like shells.
They pass me with flashes of brown skin,
clean as fields.
                    And who does not love them?
Even I who am all wilderness,
mind like a deep well,
but it will not make a boy love me
as much as one of those bare arms,
it is the despair, the pain, the delight
of no one as one of those thighs
long and wavering as young wheat.

II.

Where are all the gentle ladies?
One who wrote poems like pure fire
gone into her own oven like the witch,
pushed perhaps by the hard hand
of her own rant; one went mad;
and one said
when the magic goes you rage
unless you would be one of these.

III.
She adopted her professional name
at the suggestion of a gentleman friend
who had a mistress of that name.
She drives her own car
and frequents the chic nightclubs
in Montparnasse.
She is already a fixture at Reginés
which she alternately denigrates and applauds.

She talks vaguely of studying,
of becoming a housewife, of having children.
"You need something for the future,"
she says, slouched in her velvet sofa.
"When you see the first wrinkles around your eyes
you know. It can't last past 25."

She has modeled for Mdm. Charles de Gaulle,
vacationed at St. Tropez, and been a dinner guest
at the Rothschilds. "I think," she says
judiciously, "this may be the summit."

IV.
High on biphetamine and hunger
their voices whine like jets
taking off into some heaven
where bodies are not stretched and bent,
shot up with plastic, tightened
into the vice of agelessness,
where wrinkles and sagging pockets of skin
can be rehung gently like drapes
returned from the cleaners.

The names, Crystal Springs and Green Valley,
are their guarantees of immortality;
and Palm Springs, Miami Beach, Las Vegas;
and the young boys, prowling the boardwalks
and beaches in search of the cameras and silk shirts
that lie in their cunts as in antique chests.

V.
The only woman on the platform that night,
she read poems for all her betrayals.
At the end a note arrived from a man in the audience
offering her a good fuck, if that is what
all those poems were about.

VI.
We have all grown this wild, though once
I was tamer, one day or week
when it seemed my life was reopening
and somewhere, I think of the mountains,
working for those I love, I would have become
a gentle lady, where a body that could balance loads
was useful, these blunt fingers beautiful
for what they made; where to sleep and awaken
in a room without fear was natural,
no eyes at the windows, no bolts on the doors.

For now I may go naked, or in black like the old women
of Spain, for either would declare me
to the wilderness; that I grow old
and wait for gentleness; that I would write
for some moment of tenderness;
but that while I wait I rage

in case there is nothing more.

KEEPING SECRETS

I like it
knowing things you don't know
about me,
what I do in your absence.
Even when I am in the same room
I keep secrets,
singing to myself in the kitchen;
you ask me for coffee
because I am walking around
doing nothing
that is a secret
I keep
what I am doing
while I set the kettle on.

You tell lies but
I keep secrets so
I do not have to lie
to say what is *not* true
keeping what is true
inside
my secret

like my sex
which is a secret
inside me, and you cannot know
unless I tell you
whether I want you
or not.

TELLING ROSELLA ABOUT MY HANDS

Tonight, Rosella, I wanted
to cut my hand off.
I am not being dramatic now,
I can show you the mark.
But the knife was as dull
as my audacity
so I have little to show.

I remember telling you
only this morning,
about my hands. Now
I can tell you more.
Sometimes at night
they crawl like spiders across the bed,
leap for the window.
They want to throw themselves
through the glass
or lie under the window frame
as it closes.

> I said,
part of me is self-destructive.
That part is my hands.
I love them when they talk,
then they say more than words,
their ten letters are alphabets
without limitation.
I love them when they are in love,
touching, gentle, sweet as children
and as shy.

42

But they are no good in a crisis.
They dangle helplessly or else
twist in voiceless rage.
Then I hate them and they know it.
They run away, ready to hurl themselves
off any cliff.

I can never get love and hate straightened out
so everyone pays, my hands,
my suicides, foraging for instruments.
One turns on the gas,
the other holds the match
waiting to see what I have in mind.

BRIGITTE BARDOT: SOURED RECLUSE

> *"Allergy:* exaggerated or pathological reaction
> to substances, situations, or physical states that
> are without comparable effect on the average
> individual."

The sexpot of the sixties
is allergic to humanity.

"I see no one.
I don't go out.
I am disgusted with everything.
Men are beasts."

See how all great philosophies
sway on the point of a pin,
how all great reactions
begin with an irritant as small
as a grain of pollen
or a nodule of dust.

Does she sneeze, itch,
break out in a rash,
experience respitory embarrassment?
As one thing leads to another,
the chain reaction lashes
and links the delicate balance
of metabolism until it goes crazy.

She could have been another Mao
given the right irritant,
"without comparable effect on
the average individual."

38 years old and
her whole arm begins to swell,
the chart lights up
like a war planning board.
Mold, dust, feathers, egg yolk,
you name it.
She has named it:
                    "Men are beasts."

So reserve your pity, I tell myself,
for those who deserve it.
This is a case history
as common as the cold.
It can be cured by higher altitudes
or a dryer climate:
                    "Her fascination with men is drying up."

She has the answer for herself.
The rest of us can wait.
She has the answer.
She doesn't need any of mine.

THE WAY BACK

"Yet where I saw space devoid of
life my Eskimos saw life."
   <u>*Kabloona*</u>*—Contran de Poncins*

This is my first time on the trail back.
To watch the world, to lighten the load,
to learn the names of the dogs, this
is what you learn first. Then I watch the snow.

Snow, I learn, is not white but
a thing of endless changes,
a thing to be dealt with always,
a thing that will not tell you where you are,
a thing to build with, drink from, fight against,
a thing to ride upon. With snow you are always busy,
always watching. Always I am afraid.

*

What drives them is the instinct of destruction.
They follow the signs of birds.
They find tiny fish hidden under stones.
They scavenge broken kettles, sticks of driftwood,
scraps of wire and rope from along the shore.

The whale and the caribou are gone
but one of the women brings back a dead bird,
shot with a .22, and we eat,
we tear it apart with our hands,
eat it raw, gnaw, swallow, gulp,
alive to nothing but the passion of the feast.
The baby swallows, or tries to swallow,
a whole fish. The tail protrudes from his lips,
smiling, mouth full of raw fish and tail.

*

But there is always the moment
when we lose our way.
I see a world of nothing, but somewhere,
the man says, there is a sign,
a track of a sled, perhaps, a rock;
the only trace I see is the Eskimo,
moving in the white void,
looking for tracks, floating in the wind,
floating upon the wind, looking for signs.

He is looking for signs
known only to himself
because within 150 miles of the Magnetic Pole
the compass goes crazy; in a storm
there are no stars.
He is looking for signs
and sometimes we will turn around
just to search for these signs.

*

But the Eskimo will not give up.
He will look through his telescope
while I am freezing.
I curse him. I want to go back,
go back to something
I can understand, somewhere where
I know the signs.

"There are no signs here,"
I scream into the wind.
"It is stupid to look for signs
in this endless chaos."
But he will climb to a high point.
He will look through his bartered telescope.
He will not give up.

I am not cold so much as I am in the cold,
I *am* the cold, searching
for a non-existent issue.
"We are not going anywhere," I cry.
"We are all mad."

*

Is there another land so silent?
It can destroy you,
the line around the real world
(or what I think is the real world)
narrowing until it is no wider than my body,
my heartbeats slower.
Sometimes I must shake myself, hard,
like a deep sleeper,
to keep my heart awake.
It says: "Go where? Go out?"
As if that were nothing and
it is all there is. Cold and silence
have stopped the hands of the clock.

And the grotesque disproportion of the task
and the effort to perform it
become the fault of the cold and the silence.
They have taken everything away
and I am expected to put it back.

Who is this who pretends to be me?
And if it is me, what am I doing,
floating through dreams of ice and snow,
following an Eskimo. I have been told
"Beware of fantasies," but I must find the Eskimo.
Where is he now?
Somewhere in the cold and silence
waiting patiently to catch a seal.

*

We are poised over a seal's airhole.
We have been waiting for hours
for the feather on the line to move.
That would mean a seal had surfaced to breathe.
We are breathing. It is the only breathing,
cold smoke that hardens on our faces
until we wear white masks, the same
faces, cold and silent.

"But," I say, "I am no Eskimo."
Unless, waiting by the air hole,
he feels as I do,
as I am now, waiting as he is
for the feather to move,
to see or feel some other breathing
besides my own, freezing on my face.

*

Because his life is heavy with silence
he cannot explain himself to me.
Only what we do together
explains him to me;
that the sun is not necessary to his happiness,
that he laughs in the cold grey landscape,
that explains him to me.

He builds me an igloo in an hour
with a bone knife, sheet ice
for windows, even a small carving
to place before the door.
I tell him I admire this fact immensely
but I cannot say why. Suddenly
I cannot explain myself to him,
between us a film of hoar frost,
the inexplicable that remains unexplained.

The next day I find an Eskimo doll outside the igloo.
It has no form, it has no face,
externally without expression. Why do I feel
it broods upon some secret?
Shapeless, covered with animal hide,
tufts of animal fur stuck to the head,
it struggles to resemble something human.
This is his gift, his way of saying what he cannot say.
I sleep with it because perhaps it was meant to resemble me.

                    *

But now I must say something about my hate.
When everything was in disorder
I hated the disorder; now everything
is an order and I hate that more.
This Eskimo knows what is necessary to survive.
I know that survival is driving me crazy.
When I try to change things he smiles,
the smile of a deaf man. And when I see that smile,
that smile that neither hears nor sees,
I want to kill him.

One night (Eskimo fashion) he
gave me to another man.
In the morning I said to my new man,
this is what will make me happy. Follow
him to the seal hole. I want you to
come up behind him (Eskimo fashion)
and stab him in the back, shove
his body under miles of water and ice,
to join those seals he is always,
always waiting so patiently to rise.
Only then will I smile, knowing he will never rise.
He said he would do it, but when he got there
the hunt was good and together they brought home
much meat and made a feast. When I cried:
"You have made a feast of me," they laughed.

                    *

So he still sits here.
He knows he is an important man.
"How lucky you are," he says,
"to have me. I have the best dogs,
I am the best hunter, I know the trails."
So he still sits, drinking my tea,
telling me that he is an important man.

In the morning my other lover goes away
to follow the bear hunt he has heard of.
There are many bear in the north and he follows.
So I am left with this man whom I admired while he
                                    built my igloo,
whom I loved in the storm, but
as soon as it was over,
as soon as all was well again,
this man became for me a stranger.
He became my enemy.

                    *

And now he is in a rage. I have given him gifts.
"These things you give me are not for me,"
he says, shaking with anger.
He flings them around, knocks over the lamp,
and in the total darkness
the dogs rush into the igloo
and devour whatever is left.
He leaves the igloo but returns,
before morning, kicking the dogs out
and asking for tea, as if nothing had happened.
Then he lies down again to sleep. Later
this is all he will tell me:

"I shouldn't have started to run.
Running is the worst thing a man can do.
It makes him perspire and when he stops
he freezes. But I ran nevertheless...
I ran back where I had come from.
This is how men get lost, for they always
arrive at a different point
from that which they are running to."

*

But I love the dog who leads the team,
the dog I run ahead of as I lead them.
Running I sometimes forget where I am,
and I am in another country, or in one of my memories.
Then suddenly I will feel him next to me,
running beside me, saying:
"Go, straight on. I am with you."
Suddenly in all this infinite land,
in all this barren, cold, and silent land,
there is something that runs with me,

and we will run on
while the Eskimo
perched on his 12 hundred pounds of load,
wonders why we run, laughing and crazy,
caught up in the joy of our running.

*

Coming into the post
(if you are an Eskimo)
you want to arrive with dignity,
you want to make a good impression
even if your dogs are old and you have run
most of the journey.
You must make an entrance
with everything in place,
as if the journey had cost you nothing,
as if you were not even sure why you came.

And only then, when all of this is established,
the audience prepared,
only then may you turn around
and, like the benevolent conqueror,
descend into the waiting throng of friends,
descend into their waiting hands and smiles.

This he also tells me, just before we arrive.
*
In the igloo the baby plays,
naked among the furs, the women,
the puppies and pregnant bitches
brought in out of the cold.
He falls among the soft furs
and the warm bodies, naked
to all their touches. His sister
tosses him in the air
but he laughs, unafraid.

Later we all lie naked among the furs
in the strange light of oil lamps.
Around us, the warm breathing,
the soft stirring of the child against me,
we are whatever warmth there is,
naked and safe for a moment under animal fur.
The length of my body seems to be the length
I have traveled to be here.

Outside the dogs sleep in a tumble,
buried in snow, tails, noses,
buried as we are in the bodies of each other.
In Eskimo, the word for "reality"
means "the thing turned towards you."
I am here. There is nowhere else to turn.

*

No one really wants this place.
They are alone with it,
it is theirs and no one disputes them.
They have learned to live here
and that protects them from the cold,
the hunger, the endless drive of need,
the world that directs their march.
Yet they do not see it as a hard land
since it is theirs and they have learned to live here.
That is something I must tell myself often.
Someone has learned to live here.

WATCHING AN OLD LOVE STORY

A LEGEND

One day they told her
of a great light,
then the green
water was not
the same,

she restlessly driving
further and further
toward land
one night dreamed
the light lay
over her
covered her eyes
with yellow hair.

Awaking to trees and
grass still green
she cried until
in the east
the yellow light flashed

he was there
he was riding over her

now nothing was the same.
She watching for nine days
grew thin and supple
from following the light
and looking one morning
saw herself sun/flower
turning and bending
to catch his riding.

And he, seeing her,
saw his own face mirrored
in her anxious eyes,
saw her held now
by the land, smiled
at the happy ending.

SOMETHING TO DO WITH IT

Because it was not
love yet
it was easy to say,
it was easy loving
you because we were still finding
each other and you had not said
yet, I disappoint you.

We went to certain places
where things happened
for the first time, now
should we go back

like our rabbit
who only rolls over in
one place, the place
she did it first, thinking
perhaps that had something
to do with it.

I WANT TO BE BEAUTIFUL

with the same desperation
as a 55 year old executive
who wants to go to the moon.

He stares at his body.
He compares it with the body
he saw yesterday.
He reads it like a map
that shows both departures
and destinations.
       There is not much difference.

He thinks of the moon
which is also mapped.
He thinks of his life.

The moon is not there
except as the force
which drags and pulls his
flesh
       as impersonally as it
calls the tides.

He cannot bear his nakedness.
If he could he would
never undress or would
drag the sun into his basement.

But the moon, he would allow it
to whirl darkly, that hawk
he would let it eat him,
the pounds of flesh
falling at his feet.

And stepping out, all muscle,
an anatomical sketch,
a beautiful arm reaches up
and between those new fingers
finds the hawk's wing
    and crushes it!

MY CARD IS THE ACE OF CUPS

The strangeness of the park
this morning
is the strangeness of walking
out of winter
the strangeness of reaching
up to touch a branch
most strange is this morning
when there are only fathers in the park
and I am seeing them
not as men
but as fathers.
The wind fills the hollows
of my dress
and I wonder:
when did women learn first
that it was not the wind
sweeping in dry from the desert
that filled the hollows of their womb
but the men who lay beside them.
When did they forget this
and turn again to the wind,
the strangers who leave them hollow,
forgetting the fathers
who labor beside them.
My hand reaching for a branch
opens like a cup,
my symbol,
all hollow, receptacle,
the hollowness of women
waiting to be filled,
the cup, my quintessence,
nine months of clear water
rising steadily to the brim,
lipped over, rippling

as the moon tips and spills
always giving up its borrowed light.
Birth is not a lightening
but the heaviness of hollows,
my cup, my hand,
opening out in love.

WATCHING AN OLD LOVE STORY

In the movies
people say goodbye so
easily and with such
tragic grace.

Spring
has broken winter but
we do not part gracefully
no more than the lake ice
straining and cracking
it cannot say
as Ingrid Bergman says
"Don't touch me!
Let me go!"
with only a beautiful
cracked smile.